FRIENDLY PLASTIC FOR STARTERS
©2003 Liz Welch

Published by

RARE BIRD
61 Shelford Road
Radcliffe On Trent
Notts
NG12 1AJ

Printed in the UK

ISBN 0-9544649-0-7

The information in this book is presented in good faith, but no warranty is given nor results guaranteed.

All images in this book are created by the author.
The subject of the photography is all the authors own work.

CONTENTS

A NOTE ABOUT
FRIENDLY PLASTIC
AND CHILDREN

Children over 8 with close adult supervision love Friendly Plastic. Although the plastic is non-toxic, does not give of noxious fumes and does not get hot enough to burn if it is heated to the correct temperature, the heating devices get very hot and therefore children need close supervision to ensure that they are kept safe.

FRIENDLY PLASTIC
FOR STARTERS

FRIENDLY PLASTIC IS A MODELING material like no other I know. It softens and is pliable when it is warm, and hardens as it cools to a flexible yet strong material that can be used in a huge variety of ways. Do not expect to work it like polymer clay, and neither is it like the plastic that shrinks when you heat it. Read on and discover the unique properties of Friendly Plastic and some of the really exciting things that can be done with it. This book will lead you through your first encounter and explain what to do and how to do it. If you follow the first few pages closely you will feel confident about moving on to the projects further on.

On first inspection the modeling material is hard but flexible in it's "natural" state of seven inch strips of plastic. It is covered on one side with brightly coloured metallic foil. Cut it and warm it to 60-70°c and it becomes pliable as toffee. It can be molded, draped, cut, stamped, shaped, patched, pieced, painted, pushed and pulled, and that is just for starters. It can be used with all sorts of other media such as textiles and wood, glass and wire. Projects can be completed quickly, there is no waste and with the proper supervision children can use it too. *

The softening process takes moments in either hot water, the oven or using a heat gun. Cooling is equally quick and can be speeded up with the judicious use of a bowl of cold water. This softening and cooling process can go on indefinitely which is a great bonus if you need to leave your project half way through and return to it days or weeks later.

* Please see the note at the front of the book about working with children.

Metallic foil covers one surface of the plastic strip (there is a range of primary colours with no foil). The range of colours and patterns is fabulous, but you do not have to be restricted to the colours as they are, you can change them by adding texture, painting, or writing on the surface, repeatedly heating to dull the bright colours, distressing the surface, or by adding colour in the form of metallic waxes. You can even create your own strips by placing bits of one colour on top of a piece of another colour (or next to) and softening them together.

The reflective properties of the metallic foil means that by careful juxtaposition of colours in a design you can create an optical mixing of colours which reflect the light and pick up on the hues and tones that surround your design.

All in all it is a really exciting material that deserves a much wider appreciation. In this introductory book I intend to help you see some of the very many possibilities just waiting for you to discover. Whether you make cards or love jewellery, want to create gifts or make decorative items for the home, or use your creations in textile projects and costume, there is a technique to suit your needs. Explore, experiment, find what works for you and have fun.

Lace work box
17 cm x 10 cm x 65 cm

TOOLS AND EQUIPMENT

Many of the tools that you will find useful can be readily improvised from items around the house. Below is a list of things that you will need to get you started.

REALLY USEFUL STUFF

❖ An electric skillet of frying pan or some other means of keeping water at a temperature of 60-70°c. A shallow pan on the hob or portable electric ring also work well. To begin with use a thermometer to check the temperature until you get used to judging It

❖ A dry heat source, either the oven on the lowest setting, or ideally a craft heat gun (Not a paint stripper or a hairdryer). Heat guns can be used on just part of your design instead of the all over approach necessary with the oven. They are also an instant source of heat and are safe and easy to use.

❖ Good strong, sharp scissors for cutting the plastic strips. I have never found a Stanley knife to work for me, but do not let me put you off!

❖ A suitable work surface: A piece of 6mm window glass with the corners ground off or taped, a rubber mat (not a patch worker's cutting board as this will distort with the heat), a glass surface protector, a non-stick metal baking sheet or a Teflon non-stick mat.

Tip: Watch out for fan ovens as you might find your design rearranged by the blowing action of the fan

- ❖ Aluminium cooking foil, the thicker and stronger the better.
- ❖ Rolling pin - metal, glass, or ceramic 3cm or more in diameter. Copper central heating pipe works well.
- ❖ Bowl of cold water - and old ice cream tub is perfect.
- ❖ Towel to keep things dry as you work
- ❖ Needle tool or a needle pushed into a cork, or an awl.

ALL THE EXTRAS

The basic list of equipment can be added to with the following items that you might also find useful and in some instances essential for certain techniques.

- ❖ Rubber stamps, metal buttons and other objects for impressing designs and texture. Use objects with clear, well defined lines for best results.
- ❖ Moulds for making particular shapes - metal, resin, glass or ceramic
- ❖ Ball ended embossing tool or some other un pointed tool - necessary for lace work technique
- ❖ Metal sugar craft cutters for cutting shapes out of softened plastic
- ❖ Metallic wax e.g., Rub'n Buff, leafing pens, acrylic paints, bronzing powders
- ❖ Soldering iron - great for creating holes and texture amongst other things.
- ❖ Drill - for creating the hole in beads
- ❖ Old dentistry tools, leather working tools, screws and tool box items
- ❖ Wire mesh
- ❖ Ruler
- ❖ Palette knife or other flat bladed knife
- ❖ Bamboo skewers (not wood) - for draping technique and making beads

PREPARATION AND BASIC GUIDELINES

I T IS ADVISABLE TO PREPARE your work area carefully before you begin. Choose a surface that will be able to withstand a bit of water on it and will not melt or mark with a little heat. You can protect the area with a wipe-able cloth, but beware sheet polythene may cause the plastic to stick to it.

❖ Fill a shallow pan or electric skillet with 5-7 cm of water and heat to 60-70°c. Maintain this temperature, use a thermometer if you are unsure.

❖ Have a folded towel and a bowl or ice cream tub of cold water next to your work surface

❖ Arrange your rubber mat or glass work surface with your tools to hand and close to your heat source.

WARNING: Be Very careful not to let any water get near any electrical appliances or plugs. Protect sockets on extension cables with a plastic bag loosely wrapped around it. Keep the heat gun well away from any water that might be spilt or dripped. A circuit breaker may be used if you are worried.

USEFUL THINGS TO KNOW

❖ Plan your design, and cut your shapes using strong sharp scissors. Straight lines are easiest to manage.

❖ Soften ONE piece at a time either directly in the hot water or supported by the tin foil as appropriate to the technique.

❖ Remove from the water using the needle tool. Touch the tool to one corner (or end if the piece is a narrow strip) and draw the softened plastic out of the water and manipulate as desired.

❖ Do not try to lift the piece in the middle or it will fold up and stick to itself.

❖ To quickly cool and harden your work dip it into the bowl of cold water .This gives control and helps to reduce fingerprints from over-handling whilst warm,

❖ To keep a piece of plastic flat whilst it is softening in the water ready for stamping or cutting, use a piece of aluminium foil under the plastic when you put it in the water.

❖ The heat of the heat gun can spread out quite far so make sure your work area is protected with adequate matting or towels.

❖ Use a good thick baking sheet to transfer designs to the oven. Cut aluminium foil to be 3 or 4 cm bigger than your design and place it on the tray before arranging the design on top of that.

Tip: *You have two excellent control mechanisms for taming unruly plastic - tin foil keeps your design flat and easy to manage, and cold water instantly hardens the plastic helping to reduce fingerprint marks from over handling and controls any shaping you put in. Hardened plastic is easier to remove from tools.*

❖ Keep all tools clean and free from plastic by regularly dipping in cold water to harden the plastic and removing it by wiping on a cloth or between your fingers.

❖ Stop hands from sticking to the plastic by applying moisturiser or a little cooking oil to the finger tips.

Tip: *Avoid wearing nail polish as the plastic might stick to It*

❖ If the plastic distorts or sticks to tools when you pull it out immediately plunge it and the tool it is stuck to into cold water and snap it apart when it is hard. The piece may be able to be reworked or recycled into beads and moldings.

IMPORTANT: Do not let the water get too hot or the plastic will become too runny to work with and you will scald yourself.

FIRST STEPS

GETTING ACQUAINTED

FRIENDLY PLASTIC IS NOT LIKE any other modeling material I know, so it is very useful to begin with a little messing about and generally getting the feel of the product. When it is cold it is hard and difficult to cut in anything but straight lines with good strong scissors. When it is soft it becomes like toffee. If you have used hot water to soften it then it is easy to handle and model or shape. If you use the heat gun or the oven then it is soft and sticky and perfect for pulling about with an embossing tool. The key thing is do not over-heat it or the toffee will become like treacle and will lose colour and be almost impossible to work with. You will find it easier to handle if your own hands are not too dry, so rub a little cooking oil into your finger tips.

1   Begin by removing the hang tag if there is one, it is very difficult to remove when only an inch or two of plastic is left.

2   Cut a 1cm strip from the end of a stick of plastic and place in the water metallic foil side down.

3   After about 30 seconds touch the end of your needle tool to a *corner* and gently wave the plastic about in the water to see if it is bending and flowing. When it is just softly bendy bring it out of the water with the needle tool positioned in one corner. Transfer it directly to your fingers without letting the plastic touch the work surface, and try twisting it and pulling it to get the feel of it.

4   As it cools it will harden so put it back into the water and have another go. Try pinching, pleating, stretching and molding so you know what it feels like when it is warm and malleable, and also what it feels like when it cools and hardens. Neither the heating nor the cooling take very long. The actual length of time is dependent on the air temperature you are working in, bear this in mind if it is a very cold day and your work surface and tools are cold.

5   When you are happy with the feel of it, reheat the plastic and roll it into a ball. Drop the ball into the cold water to harden it and save it for making beads with later on.

MOLDING

Cut a piece of plastic about 3cm long across the width of the stick and lay it in the hot water to soften, metallic foil side down. Remove by touching the needle tool to the corner of the plastic and draw it out, transferring it to your fingers. Push the softened plastic into a metal, ceramic or resin mould with the foil side down. Be reasonably firm and push the plastic in so that it completely fills all the hollows of the mould leaving no air bubbles.

2   Turn the mould upside down and push down on the work surface. If you are using a metal mould this will cut the plastic shape out. If not the excess can be removed with scissors after it has cooled. Allow to cool or plunge into cold water to speed up the cooling process.

3   Remove the plastic from the mould (the needle tool may be helpful for this) and neaten up the rough edges with scissors or if there is only a fine membrane left then quickly dip the edge into the hot water and run your finger along it to push the fine membrane down. Do this one side at a time, plunging into cold water in between to avoid finger marks.

4   Colour can be added at this point either using metallic wax, acrylic paint or a leafing pen.

❖ Try using metal chocolate moulds or the resin moulds sold for use with polymer clay. Old metal or glass buttons can make very interesting moulds, but beware of shapes that undercut or you may have difficulty removing the plastic from the mould

❖ You can even make your own molds by using silicone based molding compounds which can be shaped around an object and then used with Friendly Plastic. It remains flexible so it is possible to make detailed moulds and still be able to easily remove the Friendly Plastic afterwards.

CUTTING

IF YOU WANT TO CUT intricate shapes from the plastic, it is far easier to do this when the plastic is soft. When it is cold straight lines are easiest to cut, but when it is soft, scissors are almost impossible to use so metal sugar craft cutters are the solution. Soften the plastic by submerging it on top of aluminium foil in hot water (metallic foil side uppermost)

1   Remove the aluminium foil to your work mat with the softened plastic uppermost . With a firm but swift action push the cutter into the softened plastic and remove promptly. Lubricating the cutter with oil will help to prevent sticking. Cool quickly by plunging foil and plastic into cold water.

Tip: If the plastic sticks to your tools then plunge the whole lot into cold water and the tool or cutter will snap out. This is the universal solution to sticky tools and fingers.

2   The cut out shape should now pop out with a little encouragement from your fingers. If it doesn't then scissors may be used to snip through the partially cut sections. If the cutter failed to reach more than the top surface of the plastic then it will need to be reheated as the plastic was not soft enough to allow the cutter to push right through. However only reheat the bit that needs it once the successfully cut shapes have been removed, otherwise the cut out shapes will re-soften and merge again and will also need to be re-cut.

3   Cut out shapes can be used in their own right as decoration for many projects - greetings cards, jewellery, motifs on book covers, decoration for pots etc. They can provide contrast to more freeform areas of a design, or used in layers to create your own decorated strips of plastic for further use. They can be stuck back to back for dangles and decorations for tassels and other hanging projects.

4   Try cutting small squares and embedding them in a single piece of plastic for a mosaic effect (see project Mad Mosaics)

5   Add them to the surface of beads for a knobbly textured look

6   Save all the "negative" plastic from the cut outs, that which you might of thought of as scrap. This can be used to great affect by placing it on top of another layer of plastic and softening and rolling it in to create another piece of decorated plastic to work with (see the section on Layering). It has many other uses too. Remember, nothing is wasted. Ever.

STAMPING

THIS TECHNIQUE IS WONDERFUL for creating texture and interest in a piece of work, it reduces the gloss and glitz of the plastic, helps to create an antiqued look and aids in optically mixing the colours.

1   Take a 3-4 cm strip from the stick of plastic, preferably a strong dark colour. Lay the strip metallic side up on a piece of tin foil and submerge in the water taking care not to let the plastic float off.

2   When it is softened remove the tin foil from the water and using a rubber stamp dipped in cold water or a little oil, stamp a pattern or texture onto the soft plastic. Use a firm but swift downward pressure and if going for texture rather than a particular design keep lubricating the stamp be-tween every 1- 2 impressions. Cool and dry the plastic.

Tip: If the stamp sticks to the plastic do not panic or pull the stamp out. Simply transfer the whole shebang to the bowl of cold water and the stamp will pull out as the plastic hardens.

3   To enhance the pattern or texture take a tiny bit of metallic wax on your finger and smear gently across the surface. The colour will glide onto the raised parts leaving the hollows alone. This is a very good way of optically mixing colours or blurring and softening overly strong colours. Alternatively apply gold acrylic paint to the surface and immediately wipe off. This will leave the paint in the hollows and the stronger colour of the plastic on the ridges.

4   This technique is very useful for adding texture as a contrast to smooth areas of your design. It can disguise joins in the plastic where you are seaming two pieces together to make a larger piece than can be cut from a stick of plastic. It is also very handy for quickly producing something interesting for card making.

5   Try stamping with other things that you might find around the house. Chose non porous items which are not made of plastic, for example bobbin cases, thick cotton lace, buttons, beads, chains and other objects to create texture and pattern. Use metal, ceramic or glass objects if you want to be sure that the plastic will not stick.

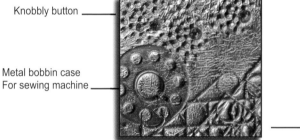

Knobbly button

Metal bobbin case
For sewing machine

Rubber Stamp

6   Do not forget that if you reheat the plastic the texture definition will be lost. Any colour you may have put on will remain, giving a lovely patterned piece of plastic which can be used any way you choose.

PIECING

Whatever you choose to make, at some point it is likely that you will want to join two pieces of plastic together. Whether you simply like stripes or want to make a box, attach an edge strip or create a checkerboard effect, joining two pieces of plastic together will become second nature to you and will crop up again and again in the following pages. See the project on PDQ Patchwork.

1   Cut two 1cm strips of plastic. To join them together hold the edge of each piece to be joined in hot water for a few seconds and then touch them together. If the strips are too narrow and your fingers find it all too much in the water, then hold one end of one strip and the other end of the second strip and dip them into the water. Now join them together by touching the sides together as shown in the diagram.

Opposite Ends Technique

If the strips are too narrow to warm the long edges without scalding your fingers, warm opposite ends in the water

Touch the softened ends of one piece to the opposite end of the next. This will tack them together ready for "sewing"

2   The join will not be permanent at this stage, but regard it like tacking, it will hold while you assemble the rest of your design.

3   To create a permanent bond the plastic must be softened on the tin foil in the water and then rolled out using your rolling pin with gentle pressure and a swift and positive action. Remove the rolling pin from the plastic every one or two rolls to allow it to cool fractionally and not to stick to the plastic.

4   Joining pieces of plastic in this way is fundamental to many projects, and particularly useful if you wish to make a box or add edges to design. In these circumstance rolling is often not possible or desirable. Instead the join is reheated gently in hot water to meld the two pieces together.

ROLLING

SOMETIMES IT IS NECESSARY TO MAKE the plastic a bit thinner before using it in a design, for instance when you wish to sew into the plastic, or make two layers back to back, or flatten out a lumpy piece (see Mosaics).

1   To do this soften the plastic by placing it on tin foil in the hot water and allow to soften. If there are two layers, join them first using the opposite ends method and then soften on foil (this will take almost twice as long).

2   Remove the tin foil from the water and using a firm but gentle and swift action roll the plastic out. If the rolling pin sticks then oil it a little but try to avoid the rolling pin being in contact with the warm plastic for too long at any one time.

3   As you roll the piece out thinner and thinner you should notice that the foil becomes duller as it begins to become stretched and more of the backing plastic shows through. This is yet another way of changing the colour intensity of the plastic.

4   You do not have to stick to smooth rollers, try textured rolling pins (the sort used for texturing clay), or the shaft of a bolt or a rubber stamp roller (see Texture Tiles Project).

Tip: If you have a pasta machine, try using it to roll the plastic. In this way much larger sheets of plastic can be made.

MODELING AND MANIPULATING

Sometimes something a little more freeform is required perhaps to simulate natural forms such as leaves or flowers. Molds will not do, and cutters are too regimented, so the only option is to go for freeform manipulation and modeling.

1   Soften a 2cm strip of plastic in hot water and remove using the needle tool by touching it to one corner of the strip.

2   Making sure that your hands are not too dry, transfer the plastic to your fingers and shape it by pulling, pinching, pleating and bending it into a pleasing abstract shape or even a flower or leaf. The aim is to do this swiftly and positively without repeatedly touching the plastic and leaving fingerprints.

3   The instant you are happy with your shape plunge it into cold water to make sure your design stays the way you made it and does not carry on drifting.

❖ For many this is the hardest technique to master as the plastic must be soft enough to manipulate, but not too soft or it will run away with you and flop everywhere. Get the temperature right and the modeling will be much easier to do. All sorts of free form shapes can be made this way, and by pinching out the edges you can achieve a fluted look which is great for flowers and leaves.

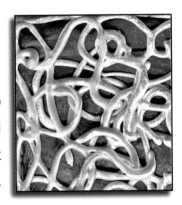

❖ Try softening different coloured pieces that you have previously joined and then manipulating these.

❖ Two strips rolled back to back look wonderful gently folded and twisted back on themselves.

❖ Edges can be coloured with paint, leafing pens or metallic wax before softening and manipulating, this is sometimes easier than trying to do afterwards.

❖ Try curling and coiling it or make long thin sausages and bend and coil them onto tinfoil like spaghetti on a plate.

❖ Make a coil by attaching a softened strip to a bamboo skewer and then turn the skewer to coil the plastic around it. This is particularly nice when using plastic strips that have been rolled back to back to give colour on both sides.

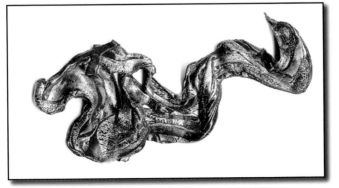

LAYERING

FRIENDLY PLASTIC CAN BE BUILT up in layers to create wonderful texture, colour and form as well as complex designs. One of the easiest ways of doing this is with the heat gun.

1   Place a piece of plastic onto tin foil on your work mat. Gather together some snippets of other colours, use up your left over bits.

2   Taking great care to heat only the plastic on the mat and not your table top, soften the plastic by holding the heat gun about 5 - 10 cm above the plastic. (Use the oven at it's lowest setting if you do not have a heat gun)

3   When the plastic is soft, you will see the edges become rounded and the high shine softens a bit. (overheat it and it will bubble and lose some colour)

4   Stop heating and very carefully place all your little snippets of plastic on top, gently pushing them into the softened plastic with the end of a bamboo skewer. Do not worry if you do not manage to place all the snippets before the plastic cools, the area can always be reheated.

5   Allow it to cool and then take the whole lot on the tin foil and place it in the hot water to soften again and confirm the bond between the layers.

6   When it is soft again you might choose to roll it gently to merge the two layers or use the end of the needle tool to swirl the snippets into the background or feather them. Of course you could stamp texture in or push the plastic into a mould, the choices are endless.

❖ This technique is used frequently to create unique multi-coloured pieces of plastic to work with further (see Mad Mosaics in the Project Pages). Specific designs can be made by placing cut out shapes or strips onto the base layer.

❖ Second and subsequent layers can also be added by softening individual small pieces in hot water and placing them onto the slightly warmed base layer and worked in to give the shape and design you desire. If this is done (placing warm plastic onto a cold layer) then it is advisable to gently re-warm the whole lot in warm water on tin foil and allow the top layers to soften gently into the lower layers. Do not leave it in the water too long or the definition and texture your have worked so hard to achieve will be lost.

❖ If texture is not the critical element in your design, then layers can be positioned on top of the base layer and carefully heated with the heat gun or in the oven (you need a steady hand to transfer a mounded pile of plastic to the oven without some pieces slithering about. I always seem to knock my tray on the oven shelf!). When it is all melted then the layers will be less definite and in fact they can be worked into with the needle tool as one might do feather icing on a cake.

Layers swirled with an icing comb and then cut out with a metal sugar craft cutter

THE   PROJECT   PAGES

T HE FOLLOWING PAGES ARE FULL of projects and ideas for you to make. Try them as they are written or work your own variations on the theme. They are designed to build upon the skills you have gathered by following the earlier Getting Acquainted pages. Please refer to the techniques sections and the tools and equipment necessary for each task. Equipment that is extra to the basic list on page five will be given.

Two necklaces made with a mixture of Friendly Plastic and bought beads. The large central bead is textured using a stamp. The round beads on the outer necklace are decorated with off cuts. The cylindrical beads are made using paper bead techniques.

Results can be achieved quickly, but if you want to be in control you need to have an understanding of how and why the plastic behaves the way it does. The best way to achieve this is to have worked through the Getting Acquainted pages without the pressure of making a particular object or project. Once you have mastered the control techniques of cold water and aluminium foil, and you are confident of the correct water temperature, then you will be able to tackle the projects without the frustration that accompanies a novice trying to learn too many things at once.

❖　Measurements for the Friendly Plastic is from the 7" x 1 ½ " stick unless otherwise stated. For example a 3 cm strip means 3 cm cut from the length of the 7" stick, no width will be given unless it differs from the natural width of the stick of Friendly Plastic.

At the end of each project there are some ideas to take you further and stretch your skills a little more. Remember to always keep in mind the basic approaches to heating and working the plastic. Plan your project and think carefully about the order of doing things and the heating method required at each stage. Make use of the Technique Summary chart to help you decide which heating method will work best for each technique.

Do not forget that everything is recyclable so there is no waste. If it doesn't work the way you expect it to, then do not panic, turn it to your advantage, go with whatever presents itself and you will learn even more about the way the plastic works. If all else fails, turn it into beads and make a necklace.

Colour can be added back in by wrapping another piece of Friendly Plastic around the bead, or with acrylic paint or a gold leafing pen. Very often the most exciting things result from the serendipity of things not going quite according to plan!

PDQ PATCHWORK
Brooch

THIS PROJECT UTILISES YOUR SKILLS at joining pieces of plastic together using hot water and a rolling pin. It is the quickest form of patchwork I know and will result in a stunning brooch for you to wear. Once you have tried the method below, experiment with some of the ideas that follow in the "And Then.." section.

EQUIPMENT AND MATERIALS

Friendly Plastic in three colours - about 3cm strips of each colour.

Bamboo skewer

Brooch pin

Strong flexible glue

Sandpaper or an abrading or roughening stone

METHOD

1   Cut strips of varying widths from your plastic and arrange these on your work surface. Place the strips side by side trying to vary width and colour and MAKING SURE that the end result is NOT symmetrical.

2   Join two pieces at a time using the "opposite ends" technique. This will result in a finger mark free pairing, giving each pair of strips time to cool and harden before moving on to the next pair. Remember to replace each pair in it's rightful position in your design before moving on to the next pair.

3   Join each pair of strips in the same manner, and continue until your design is tacked together.

4   Place your tacked design onto aluminium foil and soften in warm water. This should take no more than a minute.

5   Using the rolling pin gently roll out the plastic in the direction of the joins, not to make it thinner, but just ensure that all the seams are firmly "stitched" together. Cool the plastic and lift from the aluminium foil. Neaten up the edges with scissors leaving straight lines, it makes the next stage easier.

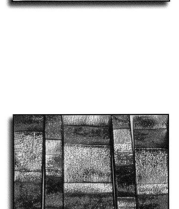

6   Cut ACROSS the sewn strips perpendicular to the seams. Cut into varying widths, some narrow some wide. Reassemble your design by taking strips (not necessarily in the order in which they were cut) and placing them head to toe next to each other to make another rectangle.

7   Tack and seam them as before in steps 2 to 7

8   Place back on the aluminium foil and re-soften in the water until good and pliable, then take a bamboo skewer and position the plastic (on the foil) over the top of the skewer

9   With a pinching and pulling motion squeeze the foil either side of the skewer, being careful not to touch the soft plastic. Pinching all the while, press down and run your fingers out along the length of the skewer, the plastic will become draped over the skewer in a gentle fold.

10   If you have time before the plastic cools and hardens,. repeat step 9 on a different part of the design. If it has hardened then you may want to reheat it to add another drape, but reheating the whole piece may result in loss of your first drape, but depending on where you have placed your first drape then it may be possible to reheat just one area and drape that.

11   Plunge the whole lot into cold water to harden the plastic quickly and keep the undulations prominent. Dry it off with a towel.

12   Run some acrylic paint or a leafing pen around the edge to finish the patchwork off and then seal the coloured side with acrylic sealant. Add a brooch pin after abrading the back of the patchwork and the pin. And leave to cure the glue for 24 hrs.

AND THEN.....

❖   Make a large sheet of patchwork and use cutters to make shapes. Use these to push into a plain background for instant framing effects. Use the bit that is left over on the top of another colour and work with a needle tool.

❖   Wrap beads with the scraps.

❖   Work your design twice, side by side at the same time and make a pair of earrings.

MAD MOSAICS
Key Ring

FORGET MESSING ABOUT WITH GROUTING and bits of tiles, this is quick and easy and very effective. Either use up all the snippets and off cuts or prepare a selection of little shapes (e.g.. squares or triangles etc.) to work with, they both look great.

EQUIPMENT AND MATERIALS

Scraps of Friendly Plastic in as many colours as you like

Two pieces of Friendly plastic about 3-4 cm square

Circular sugar craft cutter

Key ring finding

METHOD

1   Join the two big pieces of plastic back to back using the opposite ends method and place on aluminium foil, then heat with a heat gun until nice and soft, take care not to let it bubble.

2   Position the scraps in any fashion you like over the top surface (tweezers can be helpful here, but are by no means essential.) and gently push them into the softened plastic. When all are positioned, lift the whole lot on the aluminium foil and place in hot water to soften again.

3   If you wish at this point you can gently roll the scraps into the plastic using your rolling pin, this will give a smoother finish. Leaving it unrolled will result in greater texture. Soften again in hot water .

4   Cut out a neat circle using the cutter, push firmly, but remember if the cutter sticks when you try to remove it, just take the whole lot to the cold water and it will snap out when hard.

5   Pop the circle away from the excess plastic and neaten the edges by dipping in water and smoothing with your fingers.

6   When absolutely cold, turn the disc over and place mosaic side down on foil. Very gently and quickly heat just the top layer slightly. Do not over heat it or you will flatten the design on the mosaic side.

7   Using a stamp or something else that will leave an impression, gently impress a design onto the surface.

8   Cool and enhance the design with metallic wax or paint. Take the paint around the rim of the disc to finish off the piece.

9   Seal both sides with acrylic sealant. Drill a hole and attach the key ring finding.

AND THEN......

❖ Try the mosaic technique with precise shapes cut from a variety of colours. A sugar craft ribbon tool will cut lovely strips which can be cut again crosswise to give a mass of tiny squares. Arrange these using tweezers in a formal design for a more traditional mosaic effect.

❖ Create whole strips of mosaic and soften on aluminium foil and wrap around a wooden rolling pin or bottle to make a bangle.

❖ Make the base layer of plastic ultra wide by piecing strips together and rolling them. Add the mosaic layer and cut out a central aperture to make a picture frame.

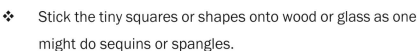

❖ Cover a glass bottle or jar with mosaic for a pretty and useful gift.

❖ Instead of off cuts or squares, use little circle, flower or leaf cut outs for the mosaic tiles.

❖ Scraps make beautiful beads.

❖ Two colour mosaics (gold on black for instance) can be very sophisticated. Add mosaic squares to just one part of a design for a more minimalist feel.

❖ Stick the tiny squares or shapes onto wood or glass as one might do sequins or spangles.

❖ Use the negative off cuts on top of another piece of plastic for an unusual abstract effect.

TEXTURE TILES
Card

SOMETIMES A SUBTLE APPROACH is required. Stamping and texturing can give wild effects, but it also lends itself to a more discreet form of decorative style. This project is simple and relies on the principle that less is more.

EQUIPMENT

two strips of Friendly Plastic each about 3cm long.

Small square metal sugar craft cutter

A large bolt or screw or something similar to give fine lines of texture.

Greetings card or card stock.

Metallic wax e.g. Rub'n Buff

METHOD

1 Using the hot water method and aluminium foil roll out the two strips of plastic to thin them a little and increase their size by approximately 50%.

2   Using the square metal cutter on softened plastic cut out five squares from each piece. (the cutter I used is about 1.5cm square)

3   Warming a few of the squares at a time on tin foil in hot water, use the bolt to gently roll a different pattern into each square, taking care not to distort the shape too much. By turning the foil and changing the angle of the bolt a good number of effects can be achieved.

4   Repeat this process for all squares. Try to leave some areas with no texture and some with a lot.

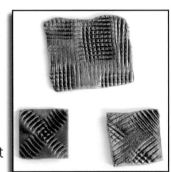

5   Allow them all to cool and then apply metallic wax VERY sparingly to the ridges and around the rim of each square. You can always add more, but you cannot take it off!

6   Seal the squares on the textured foil side with acrylic sealant. Arrange on your card (I used an uneven number - nine in total) and glue in place.

AND THEN....

❖   Texture tools can be found in the most unlikely places, the tool box is a great place to start, as is the button box. Remember that the tool needs to be almost anything other than plastic.

AND THEN....

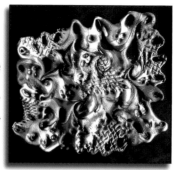

❖ Texture tools can be found in the most unlikely places, the tool box is a great place to start, as is the button box. Remember that the tool needs to be almost anything other than plastic.

❖ Texture can be added to just part of a design which gives variety and contrast, and can help hugely to tone down garish colours and optically mix that which cannot be physically mixed.

❖ Roll beads on top of an upturned rubber stamp to give a lovely textured finish.

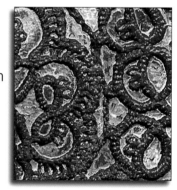

❖ Use Acrylic paint over the top and quickly wipe it off for an antiqued look.

❖ Try heavy lace and net fabrics and knobbly yarns for another wonderful source of texture.

BEADS ARE A BREEZE
Necklace

THERE ARE ENDLESS WAYS TO make beads, but one of the easiest to tackle is a simple round bead made by using up all your scraps. I use this method all the time, and it helps to keep my workspace free of small scraps which would not otherwise be useful. These beads of snippets form the basis for more elaborate beads, but I make them as I go along, tidying up the scraps and ensuring a good supply of core beads when I want to make necklaces.

EQUIPMENT

All your scraps of Friendly Plastic, the teeniest, tiniest bits can be used.

One 7" stick of Friendly Plastic

Narrow strips 2mm or so wide cut from another colour. About 10 - 12 pieces.

Hobby Drill and bracing block (see Finishing Post)

Sealant spray

METHOD

1 Divide your scraps into five piles that are approximately equal in size. If you want some of your beads to be larger than others then adjust your piles accordingly.

2 Soften them in hot water and remove using the needle tool to gather up any floating bits.

3 Roll into round beads. Keep the palm of your hand very slightly cupped as this will help to get round as opposed to elliptical beads.

4 Immediately drop the bead into cold water to harden the outside and prevent distortion. If you do not do this and simply place it on the work surface then the base of the bead will become flat and the whole lot may droop and sag and become pear shaped!

5 When all five of your piles have been made into core beads dry them off and cut your stick of Friendly Plastic into five pieces according to the size of your beads - larger for a large bead and smaller for a small bead. One 7" stick usually covers five or six beads of about 1- 2cm diameter.

7 Take one of these pieces and soften it metallic side down in hot water until it is flexible but not too soft.

8 Remove it carefully with the needle tool touched to one corner and place metallic foil down in the palm of your left hand (if you are right handed).

9 Place one of the core beads into the centre and fold up the plastic around it. Roll it in your hands until it is smooth

10 Take one or two of the narrow strips of plastic and soften them in hot water

11 Using the needle tool remove one of them and touch it to the bead. Take away the needle tool and using your fingers pull the strip gently around the bead, curving and wiggling it as you go. Small beads may only need one strip, larger beads may require two or 3.

12 When the bead has been decorated to your satisfaction roll it around for a few moments in the hot water to ensure that your decoration does not come off. Cool in cold water

13 Repeat this with all your beads. Remember these are not supposed to be identical, just similar. The beauty of these beads is in part their variation.

14 Finish your beads by drilling holes in them and sealing them. (see Finishing Post page 41)

15 Select some bought beads and arrange your design on a towel or something soft to stop the beads from rolling away.

16 Begin threading the beads onto the thong, I always start with the central bead and build the design symmetrically on either side. Tie a knot in the thong just above the last beads to stop them sliding up the thong.

17 Add beads to the very ends (for interest) and secure them there with knots on either side.

AND THEN....

❖ Beads can be used for hundreds of different things, add them to tassels, use them as tassel tops, make key rings and light pulls, use them for fancy buttons on bags, or thread them onto elastic and use as hair accessories. What you choose to decorate the beads with is without limit, scraps of mosaic, or PDQ patchwork, tiny cut out stars or circles, textured with rubber stamps, painted or drawn with leafing pens, the list goes on.

❖ They look very attractive when set off against shop bought beads.

❖ Remember if you use leather thong to thread them onto then make sure you drill the hole wide enough and buy spacer beads with a big hole.

TECHNIQUE SUMMARY

THE FOLLOWING CHART GIVES A quick reference guide for the appropriate heating method for the various techniques covered so far in this book. It is not definitive in that you can do most things with any of the heating methods, but the suggestions made give you the easiest ways of working with Friendly Plastic. After a while you will develop you own preferred way of working, and that is as it should be, but until then keep in mind the fundamental question - Will a dry heat or a wet heat serve your purpose best.

There are other techniques that I use not listed in the chart which will be dealt with in subsequent publications, for example lace work, laminating textiles and more extensive jewellery techniques.

Techniques Summary Table

TECHNIQUE	HOT WATER 60-70°c	OVEN Lowest setting	CRAFT HEAT GUN	NOTES
Piecing and Patchwork	Piece / join	To meld together	To meld together	Aluminium foil useful to stabilise
Cut Outs	Yes	Yes but with lubricant (water or oil)	Yes but with lubricant (water or oil)	Use metal cutters
Construction	Yes	No	Possible	Think before you act
Molding	Yes The best and easiest way	Suitable for some moulds but not all	Suitable for some moulds but not all	Foil not necessary
Draping	Yes	Yes	Yes	Foil useful when using dry heat
Stamping	Yes	Yes, use oil or water to lubricate stamp	Yes, use oil or water to lubricate stamp	Foil useful to stabilise, but not essential
Layering	Yes Softening the new layer for freeform shapes	Yes. Take care layers do not slip when transferring to oven	Yes Softens base layer ready for next layer. Great for swirling two layers together	This is a combination technique requiring both methods of heating for some items
Wrapping	Yes, best method for small items	OK but not brilliant	OK but not brilliant	Tin foil useful especially with larger items
Beads	Yes	OK for non rolled or wrapped beads	OK for non rolled or wrapped beads	Use _bamboo_ skewers for wrapped beads. Drill holes in cold hard beads with craft drill

None of the techniques in this chart should be considered only in isolation, they can be combined in a variety of ways. Just think a little about which heating method is going to suit your ends for each stage of the process, dry sticky heat, or wet malleable heat. For example you could work a piece of patchwork (wet heat), cut out shapes wet heat), use the shapes for decorating a box (dry and/or wet heat), and drape the "negative" remainder over a bowl to make an open-work dish (wet heat). Embellish it further with the layering techniques (dry and wet heat). A bit of thought before you begin will greatly assist you in completing your project with the minimum of difficulty.

A LITTLE EXTRA HELP

HERE FOLLOWS A HOST OF tips, the sort of thing I wish someone had passed on to me when I started using Friendly Plastic. I am sure that it will not take you long to discover some really useful tips and tricks yourself, and if you do, then why not pass it on to someone else. We will all benefit from learning from one another, you never know, someone else may pass on just the bit of help that you were looking for.

❖ If you do not want things to slip and slide then use a dry heat method. For example the first layer of any pulled work is best done with dry heat. Subsequent layers can be added piece by piece after softening them in hot water.

❖ 3D construction is best done with only the relevant part being warmed, therefore the ability to dip only the bit that needs to be joined into the hot water makes the most sense. The oven or the heat gun may warm too much of the piece and make the whole thing flexible and soft instead of only one small part.

❖ For large 3D pieces shaped around a former, a deep pan of water is better than a shallow pan.

❖ Stamping is easier when there is plenty of lubricant, therefore the hot water method is best, but you can use dry heat and keep dipping the stamp into water or oil before making each impression.

❖ Small items are easily wrapped if they have been heated using water. Larger items can be wrapped around objects if they are stabilised with aluminium foil. In which case either dry or wet heat can be used.

❖ Remember to use aluminium foil when you need to keep your piece flat and undistorted, for example when you wish to stamp or cut out pieces.

❖ Freeform shapes and plastic for molding is far better done without the hindrance of aluminium foil. After all the plastic is going to be handled and manipulated so you do not want the plastic stuck to a bit of aluminium foil.

❖ Bead making involves many different processes but by and large the easiest way to work Is with hot water. The exception being for beads that are cut out, or beads that are laminated with fabric. The former can be done with dry heat, but the latter must be done with dry heat.

❖ Remember that nothing is wasted, everything can be recycled.

❖ The water temperature should be around 60 -70°C. If it is hotter then you will find the plastic very hard to control. If it is cooler you will wait a long time before you can work it!

❖ Heat guns are brilliant but do take care to clear the area of everything but the bit of plastic you wish to soften.

❖ Although there are many different colours available in Friendly Plastic, do not be afraid to change them to suit you by adding metallic wax, paint, leafing pens etc, or giving plenty of texture to dull down a garish area.

❖ You can create your own colours by joining sections of all your off-cuts and swirling them together. The resultant piece can be treated as just another stick of plastic to work with.

FINISHING POST

ONCE YOU HAVE CREATED YOUR masterpieces you might want to know how to finish them off ready for use. Just how do you attach jewellery findings and make holes for threading; should the fragile foil surface be protected in any way; which glue should you use; how do you attach beads; is it washable; how should it be looked after? The following suggestions may help to answer some of these questions.

Sealant

The foil on the surface of the plastic will rub off if it is constantly being chafed, for example beads on a necklace rubbing against clothing, or a light pull used to turn on and off a lamp. To protect the foil spray all work that will be touched or worn with an <u>acrylic</u> sealant available from DIY stores and artists supplies. Make sure you use acrylic sealant and not a solvent based one. They are available in gloss, satin and matt finishes, the choice is yours. Use a spray box made out of an old cardboard box and ventilate the room well, or take the box outside to spray. Spray once according to the instructions on the can, leave the sprayed items to dry, and then turn them around and spray again. Repeat this turning and drying process until the items are covered completely.

Note: One sided items like brooches or pieces that are to be attached to cards for example, only need to be sprayed on the decorative side. It may hinder the gluing process if the reverse is sprayed.

Glue

Always a tricky one in the UK as all the best glues for the job seem to be in the US. The glue needs to stay clear and flexible and not go yellow or brittle. It is also useful if it can fill in any dips and hollows.

A good place to look for suitable glues is in model shops.

My glues of choice are:

Goop (USA), E6000 (USA), Victory 1991 by Bond (USA) UHU Power (UK)

Given the choice I use one of the first 3, but I am very keen to find a UK supplier of glue that does the same job just as well. Unfortunately neither the hot glue gun or Super Glue work well enough. Follow the instructions on the tube, but most of these glues require 24hrs to properly cure before you can be confident that things will not start falling off.

Holes

Holes in beads cannot be made easily while the plastic is still warm, the plastic distorts if you try to push a needle tool through it. The neatest way is to use a hobby drill. Take a short piece of four by four gate post or similar chunk of wood. Chisel out a shallow dip in one end and fill it with Plasticine or Blue tack. Place the bead firmly into the Plasticine and bring the drill down while gently holding the bead. The Plasticine keeps the bead steady and prevents it whizzing around the drill bit. It is also a great help when trying to drill small beads when your fingers get very close to the drill. The drill bit will get rather clogged up with plastic, but every bead or two simply pull off the excess plastic and save it for recycling into another bead. If you have one, use a bench drill instead of the hand drill, it is much easier to control and get a vertical hole.

An off cut from a gatepost makes a good holder for beads and small objects for drilling. Gouge out an indentation and fill it with Plasticine. This will help to hold the bead while drilling.

Abrasion

This roughening up of the surface to be glued is necessary when attaching jewellery findings, or you will find that your earrings and brooches drop off the studs and pins when you least expect it! Rub both the finding and the plastic with a piece of sandpaper or special abrasion stone (eg carborundum) before applying the glue.

Attaching Beads

This has to be the most commonly asked question of all. Can you add beads to a project by pushing them into softened plastic? The answer is generally "not permanently". However the bead can be pushed in to provide an indentation, and when the plastic is cool, prize the bead out and then glue it in. This way you will avoid nasty surprises of beads dropping off in cool weather! The plastic will continue to expand and contract with changes in temperature, this growing and shrinking process may be just enough to loosen a carefully placed bead. Be safe, Glue it in.

The exception to this rule is when the bead or sequin is pushed in far enough into the warm plastic for the plastic to rise up through the hole and around the sides, thus securing the bead in place. If this has happened then do not try to remove it to glue it, you may damage your design.

Some tiny beads have no holes (Accent Beads). These can be embedded in the plastic by rolling the warm plastic in the beads, or pushing them in with your fingers or a too. Many will stick, but those that do not can be reapplied with glue. Treat these tiny beads like chunky glitter and sprinkle liberally into the warm plastic, push them and roll them in. Alternatively use a soldering iron to pierce the foil surface and reveal the sticky plastic underneath. Sprinkle on the beads and push in. Cool the plastic naturally (without the aid of water) and brush off the excess for re-use. Spray sealant will help theses tiny beads to stay in place.

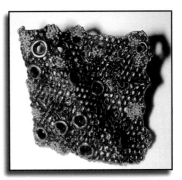

Brooch embedded with tiny Accent beads that required no glue.

After Care

Your beautiful masterpiece is finished. Enjoy using it. Jewellery can be perfectly safely worn in the heat of an Australian summer let alone a British one where the temperature generally does not reach 30 degrees let alone 60 -70 degrees centigrade. However, beware; do not leave your work in the car, whilst it is parked in the sunshine, the temperature in an enclosed car can be hot enough to melt a biro let alone a piece of Friendly Plastic!

Ironing something with Friendly Plastic on will result in a gooey mess. Do not do it!

Washing at 40 degrees is not hot enough to harm the plastic but the abrasive action of tumbling fabric will dull the shine even with a sealant. The water will eventually manage to penetrate the seal and get underneath. It will lift, go milky and look nasty. Avoid washing in washing machine if you can. Hand washing very gently and infrequently will be OK.

END PIECE

I HOPE YOU HAVE ENJOYED working through this introductory book on Friendly Plastic. I have had many happy years of experimenting with this amazing modeling material, and I am convinced that there are still many new ways of working with it that I have not yet discovered. If you discover something, please do share it. The more people who use it the more ideas that will be generated for each and everyone of us to try. If you would like to share your ideas and experiences you may post messages on my web site and submit images for the gallery pages.

www.rarebird.co.uk
rarebird@dial.pipex.com

Mail Order
Rare Bird, 61 Shelford Road, Radcliffe-On-Trent, Notts NG12 1AJ
Tel: 0115 9336268

I stock most the colours of Friendly Plastic, themed packs plus tools, heat guns, rubber mats, Rub n Buff, Accent beads, metal cutters, rubber stamps, and more. The Web site has projects and gallery pages plus a links page.

The more we share the more we learn, the more we give the more we grow